DEADLY GAME

Written by Tom Bradman

Illustrated by Kaley McCabe

RISING ★ STARS

ISBN: 9781398325579

Text © Tom Bradman
Illustrations, design and layout © Hodder and Stoughton Ltd
First published in 2022 by Hodder & Stoughton Limited (for its Rising Stars imprint, part of the Hodder Education Group)
An Hachette UK Company
Carmelite House, 50 Victoria Embankment, London EC4Y 0DZ
www.risingstars-uk.com

Impression number 10 9 8 7 6 5 4 3 2 1
Year 2026 2025 2024 2023 2022

Author: Tom Bradman
Series Editor: Tony Bradman
Commissioning Editor: Hamish Baxter
Illustrator: Kaley McCabe/Advocate Art
Educational Reviewer: Helen Marron
Design concept: David Bates
Page Layouts: Rocket Design (East Anglia) Ltd
Editor: Amy Tyrer

The publishers would like to thank the following for permission to reproduce copyright material.
Chapter heads © benjaminlion/AdobeStock.

With thanks to the schools that took part in the development of *Reading Planet* KS2, including: Ancaster CE Primary School, Ancaster; Downsway Primary School, Reading; Ferry Lane Primary School, London; Foxborough Primary School, Slough; Griffin Park Primary School, Blackburn; St Barnabas CE First & Middle School, Pershore; Tranmoor Primary School, Doncaster; and Wilton CE Primary School, Wilton.

A catalogue record for this title is available from the British Library.

Printed in the United Kingdom

Orders: Please contact Hachette UK Distribution, Hely Hutchinson Centre, Milton Road, Didcot, Oxfordshire, OX11 7HH.

Telephone: (44) 01235 400555. Email: primary@hachette.co.uk.

MIX
Paper from
responsible sources
FSC™ C104740

CONTENTS

CHAPTER 1

Light from the screen flashed in Jay's eyes. The figure he was controlling ran through the jungle, dodging from side to side. The alien attacks were easy to avoid, just distractions. The goal was close.

His fingers skipped from button to button, the controller held tightly in his hands. He felt it in his bones, tasted it in the dryness of his mouth. A few more seconds and the cannons would be ready. A few more seconds and he'd win. He'd beat Dad!

He risked a glance around the living room. Mum looked up from her phone and gave him most of a smile. Dad was on the sofa, using the tablet to play against him but looking half asleep.

Jay was about to give him a surprise.

Jay focused on the game. He saw Dad's fortress ahead. His dad had built a castle, trusting walls to save him. Jay was into movement and tactics though, and he knew how to knock down a few boring walls. He'd got control of the battle satellite as soon as the game had started.

It was all about timing. Any second now and the satellite's cannons would be fully charged ... they'd fire, and he'd go through the hole they'd make — and win.

He moved through the trees, lining up his run with split-second accuracy. He charged up a ramp and was leaping through the air towards what was about to become a smoking breach in the fortress walls.

He fired the cannon.

The screen flashed pure white, then went blank.

"What? I don't ..." Jay started to say.

"I had the satellite from the start, kid," his dad said from the sofa. "It was aimed at you the whole time. You just shot yourself."

GAME OVER slid across the screen.

"How about another game?" asked Jay. "I almost had you that time."

"You weren't even close," Dad answered, already standing up. "And I've got too much to do."

"Maybe next time, eh?" said Mum. "Wouldn't you rather have some of your birthday cake?"

Dad looked restless and muttered to himself as he glanced at his watch.

"Come on," Mum said to Jay. "It's your favourite. The chocolate caterpillar cake. You've always loved it. We'll have a slice each, open your presents, then you can get back to your game."

"Fine," Jay mumbled, following his parents into the kitchen.

He took his place at the counter and tried to look pleased while they sang 'Happy Birthday' to him. He saw his dad checking the time again. Jay blew out the candles but didn't bother making a wish. Dad wasn't going to hang around, so why wish for something that wasn't going to happen?

Next were the presents. A new tablet, a smartwatch and loads of clothes. He didn't want to be impressed by it, but he couldn't help getting excited, ripping the packaging off everything.

Then it was over and Mum was putting away the plates while Dad stuffed wrapping paper into the recycling bin.

"Just one more game, Dad?" Jay asked. "It's my birthday. You have to."

"I'm sorry, kid," came the answer. He was already looking at his phone, scrolling through emails. "I've got too much work."

"Come on," wheedled Jay. "I'll let you choose the game mode?"

"I told you I'm busy," Dad answered, his voice tight. "I don't have time today."

Jay grunted. "You never have time."

"Where do you think this comes from?" his Dad snapped, grabbing the new tablet, Jay's present, and holding it up. "Who do you think has to pay for all of this?"

"Leave him alone, Mike," Mum cut in. "He's a kid. Let him be a kid."

"Fine, fine," sighed Dad. "I'm sorry, Jay. I ... I need to work, okay?"

"Whatever," Jay murmured. There was a tightness in his chest that he was trying to push down.

After Dad had gone upstairs to his office, Jay's mum sat next to him and took his hands in her own.

"It's not you. He's having a hard time with work," she said, looking straight into his eyes. "He loves you. He really does. He's just stressed."

"It doesn't matter," Jay replied, not looking at her. He pulled his hands away and gathered up all his presents. "It's fine. I'll do whatever."

He left her sitting there and took all of his new stuff to his room. He didn't know what to do with it, so he dumped it on his desk and lay on the bed.

Jay closed his eyes. He'd been practising on that game all week, knowing he'd get to play Dad. He'd done his research, reading up on how to win, finding out about the satellite. Finding out how to impress Dad. Dad the games designer. Dad, who'd won awards for his games, who'd started his own company when he was a teenager. Jay felt stupid.

After a while, there was a knock on his door. It opened a crack and his mum peered around the side of it.

"I've got to go out for a bit," she said. "I wanted to check that you are okay."

"I'm fine," he answered, rolling on to his side and turning his back on her. He heard her walk into the room and felt the bed shift as she sat down next to him.

"What's the point of working so hard if you never get to enjoy it?" he whispered.

"You don't know what it's like to have nothing, Jay," she told him. "We didn't always have money. Neither of us want you to know what that's like."

"I only wanted to have fun," he whispered.

She sighed.

"Your dad's company is in trouble," she said. "We didn't want to tell you, but, well ... he could lose it all. It's this new system."

"What's going on?" he asked, sitting up and looking at her.

"I don't know the details," she went on.
"There's a new brain-computer interface.
It was all going so well. Then it suddenly
wasn't. There are play-testers. They're
kids really, but a bit older than you. They've
become trapped — hooked into the game.
They can't wake up and no one knows why.
They might die. Your dad is trying to save
them and his company. He's taken it all on
to himself."

"I had no idea," Jay whispered. "I thought
he was just busy, you know?"

"Yeah, well, now you do. I'm sorry. It's your birthday. You shouldn't have to deal with this. How about when I get back, we make some popcorn and watch a film?"

"That sounds good, yeah."

"I love you," she told him, kissing him on the forehead and getting up. "I'll only be a couple of hours."

"Love you, too," he replied.

Then he was alone again. He heard the front door close and knew that it was just him and Dad in the house. His dad would be in his office upstairs, working hard to save everything. Jay wished he could help. He felt useless, worse than useless. He'd been thinking about himself and only making things more difficult for Dad.

He had to do something. That's what Dad would do. Be active. He had to try to make things better.

He found himself tiptoeing along the corridor, trying to be quiet, and forced himself to stand up straight, walk properly. He didn't want to hide. He knocked on the study door.

"Dad?" he called out, his voice cracking a little.

No answer.

He pushed the door open and saw his dad at the desk, his back to the door.

"Dad?" he said again. "I'm sorry."

No response.

There were wires leading from the computer to his dad's head, attached to a headset that was tight on his skin. As Jay got closer, he saw that Dad's eyes were open, staring at nothing, empty.

"Dad?" he shouted. Jay grabbed his shoulders and shook him. Dad was breathing, but he didn't react at all.

On the desk, on top of the keyboard, was a piece of paper with Dad's messy hand-writing scrawled across it.

Sheryl. I've gone into the game. I can't help them from outside and I can't not try. I know it's a risk, but there's no other choice.

I love you both. X

CHAPTER 2

Jay couldn't stop looking at his dad's face
— empty, like some life-sized action figure.
Dad was trapped, just like the kids his mum
had told him about.

He grabbed Dad's phone off the desk,
knocking another set of wires with a
headset attached on to the floor. He called
his mum, but it went straight to voicemail.
She never answered when she was driving.
Well, being careful wasn't going to do any
good now. He needed help.

No, he didn't. He needed to help.

That was why he'd come in here in the first
place. To help Dad.

And what would Dad do? If it was Jay in
trouble, he'd act. He'd dive right in. He'd
attack the problem head on. And that was
what Jay should do, what he had to do.

He saw the headset he'd knocked on to the floor. It was exactly the same as the one on his dad's head. A quiet voice from somewhere inside told him not to, but he snatched the headset and put it on before the voice could grow.

Nothing for a second.

Then it got tight, squeezing his skull. A million pinpricks attacked his scalp and he screamed.

The world flashed pure white and then went blank.

He fell to the ground with a thump, but it wasn't the polished wooden floor of his dad's study. Somehow, there was grass underneath him and warmth on his face.

He opened his eyes to see shafts of brilliant sunlight coming down through the green leaves of the trees that surrounded him — some kind of forest on a summer's day. He heard birdsong and the wind sighing between the branches.

It was all so real but fake at the same time, like someone had put a filter over the whole world to make it shine more.

Very cool, Dad, he thought, standing up. Looking around, the detail was incredible, life-like, but not quite.

He could feel the breeze on his cheeks. He plucked a blade of grass out of the ground and felt the texture with his fingers, let the scent of it fill his nose. Very cool indeed.

First things first, he thought. *Find Dad.* But which way should he go? Every direction looked the same.

"Hello?" he yelled. "Heeee-llllooooo-oooh."

Nothing.

"Right, so this is a game," he told himself. "And I'm on level one, I guess. There must be something here ..."

There was a rustle behind him and he spun around. Something had moved in a bush a short distance away, but it was still now. He crouched low, moving forwards carefully, trying to peer into the shade beneath the leaves.

Sunlight glinted off something metal and sharp with too many legs. It hissed and skittered towards him, a vicious-looking mechanical spider, the size of his hand. He tried to step back, tripped, landed on his back, and panicked, pushing himself backwards, away from it.

It was fast and already jumping on to his foot, crawling over his trousers, up his leg. When it reached his stomach he saw needle-like fangs, hungrily clicking together, under dozens of glass-bead eyes. He screamed, grabbed it and threw it aside. It landed perfectly on all eight feet and immediately started running back to him.

This was it. In a flash, Jay knew what had happened to those other kids, the ones his mum had told him about. The

ones who would never wake up.
This thing had attacked them.

He wouldn't let it happen to
him.

Jay jumped up. When the spider-
thing came close, he stamped on it, hard.
Then again. And again. After the third time,
it stopped twitching and became nothing
more than a collection of metal junk.

"Not so cool, Dad," he muttered to himself.

The sun didn't feel as warm now, and he
couldn't hear the birds over the sound of
his heart beating in his chest. He looked
up and there was another spider-thing
sitting on a tree branch in front of him. It
hissed like the other one had, but
suddenly there was hissing from
all around and above. Over his
head, hundreds of metal spiders
watched him.

One jumped and landed on his shoulder. He smacked it and it fell off, and he was running, sprinting, desperate to get away. They were everywhere, leaping at him, chasing him, hissing at him.

It got dark and cold suddenly, night falling in the blink of an eye. Moonlight made the world black and white and full of shadows. He stumbled and fell, got up, pushing more of the things off himself. He kept running, gulping down lung-fulls of air.

The forest ended and Jay found himself dashing between old, beaten-up buildings, broken glass cracking under his shoes. He risked a glance behind and caught a glimpse of a carpet of the machine-things following him, rushing after him. His knees went weak at the sight and he tripped again, then dragged himself up. He didn't know where to go, only away from those things.

Brick walls with broken windows loomed overhead. One of the spiders leaped from above. By the time he thought about dodging it was too late. It landed on his arm and instantly bit deep, a shock wave of agony passing through him. He cried out and knocked it away before staggering on.

What was happening? This was a game, it shouldn't hurt! Not like that. His arm throbbed, and a coldness spread from the bite, up and down his arm. He rubbed it with his other hand, but the skin was numb and he couldn't feel anything.

He stumbled around a corner and saw them. Hundreds, thousands of the spiders, eyes all fixed on him, silent, still and watching. There were more behind. They were everywhere, all around.

There was no escape.

He fell to his knees as the cold crept through his skin.

And then there was light — headlights — and a loud horn, the sound of an immense engine, roaring and echoing in the narrow street. A truck screamed round a corner up ahead. As it charged down the street towards him, bolts of blue and green energy

shot out of makeshift weapons attached to its metal skin, frying the spiders.

Brakes screeched and the whole vehicle spun around, knocking the wall on one side, the bricks disappearing in a shower of pixels. The truck stopped barely metres from where Jay knelt in the street. A door flew open and he squinted up into harsh, white light.

"What are you waiting for?" someone shouted down at him.

CHAPTER 3

"Have you been bitten?" the girl demanded, wide eyes checking him over.

He'd been pulled into the truck as soon as he'd stood up. It was a cramped metal cabin, but big enough for him and the three other kids to move around a bit. He could see a boy up front, driving and muttering to himself. Another was digging through cases full of dirty-looking gadgets. Then there was the girl, crouching in front of him.

"They're still coming!" the driver yelled.

"Just get us out of here, Baz," the other boy shouted. "I've never seen so many of them."

"I said, have you been bitten?" the girl repeated, pulling Jay's attention back.

"Yeah, uh, one of them ..." he answered. He rubbed his arm where the spider had punctured the skin. The numbness had reached his shoulder. "It's so cold."

"Quickly, King," she told the kid rooting through the boxes.

"Yeah, yeah. Nearly found it ..." he replied. Then he was waving an enormous needle. "Okay, got it."

"What's your name, newbie?" she asked.

"Jay," he told her.

"Well, I'm Irene, and that kid who's about to stab you with the massive needle ..."

Before he could twitch away, the needle was in his arm.

He couldn't feel the injection, but warmth spread quickly through his skin and muscle. Feeling returned.

He flexed his fingers. It was hard to remember that this was a game, not the real world. The pain had been real enough.

"... he's King," she continued.

"And that's Baz up there, driving," Irene said, nodding her head in his direction.

"What's going on?" Jay asked, rubbing his arm. "Those spider-things, why were they after me?"

"Later," she told him. "First, what's your birthday?"

"It's today, April 6th," he said. "Why?"

"Happy birthday. What's your cat's name?" King shot at him.

"Cat? I don't have a cat," Jay answered.

"When was your last test at school?" Irene asked.

"Last week, history. I failed, okay?"
He shouted the answer at them. This was getting stupid. He was here to help Dad, not to get quizzed by some kids. He got to his feet carefully as the truck bounced around.

"Thanks for fixing my arm," Jay said. "But it's your turn to answer questions. What's going on?"

"Okay," King replied, hands up in surrender. "You seem fine. Shame about the cat though. I like cats."

"We had to make sure you weren't controlled," Irene explained. "One spider bite and when the cold reaches your brain, game over. 'Controlled' is Baz's word, by the way."

"I saw this super scary film once," the driver shouted. "Everyone was having their brains taken over by computers. They called *them* 'controlled'. Great film, classic."

"I'll give it a miss," Jay shouted back. "Is that what's happening here? Is that why the play-testers can't escape?"

"There used to be more of us," Irene told him. "Twenty kids — all bright, all gamers, hired to check out the new system."

"Now there are just us three," King added. "And you just got the last shot of antivirus. If you see any other kids, run!"

"I don't get it," Jay said, to himself as much as the others. "I mean, why control the players at all? What's the point?"

"No idea," Irene replied. "We've been stuck in here just trying to survive, looking for a way out. We haven't had time to rest, let alone work out what the big, evil plan is."

There was a screech as Baz hit the brakes and everyone was thrown forwards.

"Uh, guys," Baz said in the sudden silence. "We've got a problem. A major problem."

Jay and Irene climbed into the front with Baz to look through the windscreen. The headlights were bright, showing them a muddy road through a thick forest and, ahead of them, blocking the way, was a line of children. The other play-testers. They stood silently, staring at them. Then, together, they started walking slowly towards the truck. The rear-view mirror showed more behind.

"I can't just drive through them, you know?" Baz was almost crying. "They were my friends."

"There's no escape," King whispered.

"Not helping," Irene snapped.

"We will control you all," King wheezed.

The other three turned to look at King in shock, at the mechanical spider attached to the side of his head, its fangs deep in his scalp. At the emptiness in his eyes.

Jay couldn't move. He was trapped, rooted to the spot, every muscle in his computer-generated body frozen in fear. The spider must have jumped on board when they stopped for him, and hidden, waiting for the right moment. Was it his fault?

"You will become part of us," King hissed.

Growling, Baz leaped from his seat and barrelled into King, knocking them both out of the door. They hit the dirt outside and Jay could only watch as they were immediately covered in a swarm of metal spiders.

Irene was shouting at Jay.

She was telling him to run, pulling his arm.

They jumped together, from the door, over the boys and the spiders, landing on their feet and dashing between trees.

They ran. Jay heard the hissing all around, but this time there were people, too, controlled play-testers. Swift figures trying to get around and ahead of him and Irene, to trap them.

Then the sound of water. Lots of water.

The trees disappeared and they were at the top of a cliff, nothing ahead except an enormous drop into a fast-moving river below. Nothing behind except the spiders and the controlled.

"Not cool at all," he muttered.

They both jumped over the edge.

CHAPTER 4

Water hit him like a sledge-hammer, forcing the air from his lungs. He was underwater, spinning, not knowing which way was up. The 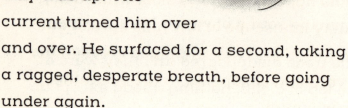 current turned him over and over. He surfaced for a second, taking a ragged, desperate breath, before going under again.

Something bumped into him, and he grabbed hold. There was rough bark under his fingers and he surfaced holding a thick branch. It helped him float and he saw the riverbanks rush past as he was carried along.

Someone was struggling ahead, kicking and splashing. Irene. He watched her go under before bobbing up again. Jay's legs were exhausted, but he clumsily swam towards her, eventually helping her hold the branch so she could get her breath back.

"Thanks," she gasped.

The sun came up as they drifted downstream. The heat was intense, and steam rose from the water. Sandy, brown cliffs appeared on one side, while a dry, dusty landscape of low hills spread out on the other. They managed to reach the riverbank, collapsing in the steaming, crusty mud.

"I don't understand," Jay said, letting the sun dry him. "How is it day? It only got dark, like, an hour ago."

"This is a game, remember?" Irene replied.

"Not the real world. One part of the forest is always dark and scary. Another is always light and beautiful. Whoever designed it went for the easy option there."

"I don't think 'easy' is the word," Jay told her, feeling like he had to defend his dad. "This is so much more than any game I know."

"No game I ever played killed my friends before," she fired back. "Come on. We'd better get moving."

They followed the river, trudging along under the hot sun. He didn't know what to say. How could he tell her that he had to find his dad, the person who had made this nightmare in the first place? He knew what Dad would say. Just get it done.

"Look," he started. Then bang! Something had hit him. Or he'd hit something. Like walking into a wall. "Ow!"

There was nothing there, just empty space in front of him. He put his hand up and it was like a pane of glass — smooth, hard, solid. He squinted and realised it was some type of screen, but way more realistic than any TV. If he stared hard enough, he could just make out the bumps of pixels on the horizon.

"What is it?" asked Irene.

"It's hard to see," he said. "But there's a screen here. Put your hand up."

She ran her fingers over whatever it was.

Behind them there was a low rumble that quickly grew into thunder. Jay turned to see a giant monster made of stone dragging itself violently out of the ground. The creature roared and took a step forward. They backed away but found themselves trapped by the screen.

"What do we do?" Jay asked. His hands were feeling for a way through, but there was nothing. This couldn't be it. It couldn't end here.

Every step the monster took made the ground shudder and kicked up a cloud of dust. Every thud from its feet sounded huge and unstoppable.

He'd failed. He hadn't helped. He hadn't even found Dad.

"I don't know what to do, do I?" Irene said. She'd picked up a stone as a weapon, but threw it aside, knowing it was useless.

"We have to do something!" Jay yelled. "I have to find my dad!"

The creature stopped.

"Jay?" it rumbled.

"How do you ...?" he answered.

Stone skin fell away and sand billowed out, fading to reveal his dad, standing on top of a pile of rubble.

They ran together and hugged.

"I'm so sorry, kid," Dad said. "I couldn't see you with all that stone on. I thought you were attackers. What are you doing here?"

"I came to help," Jay said. It felt silly to say it. All he'd done so far was run from one disaster to the next.

"You shouldn't be here, Jay," Dad replied, holding him at arm's length. "It's too dangerous. And who's this?"

"I'm Irene," she said, keeping her distance. "You?"

"Mike," he said. "I'm Jay's dad and I'm going to fix all this. Come on, if you're here, I'd better show you what's going on."

He took a small disc out of his pocket and squeezed it. Suddenly, beyond the invisible wall, out of nothingness, appeared a massive, shiny factory. Hundreds of pipes led into giant, silver buildings. Lights flashed. Machines clicked and clacked. Everything hummed with energy and power.

"Very cool, Dad," Jay said.

"I know, right?" he agreed. "Built it all myself."

"How did you build all this?" Irene asked.

"Didn't Jay tell you?" Dad answered. "This is my game. I designed it all and now I'm going to put an end to it."

"You what? You designed this nightmare?" she shouted, the words exploding out of her mouth, her pointed finger jabbing into his chest. "My friends are dead and you're acting all proud."

"Woah," Dad said, holding up his arms. "No one's dead! The system is just using their brains. I programmed the system to always try to improve. To do that, it needs more computing power. It's trying to tap into the greatest computers in the universe — human brains! They're still alive, I promise."

"So that's why it's controlling the play-testers?" Jay asked.

"Exactly," his dad said. "But I can free them. I've made a virus that'll shut everything down and get everyone home. I only need to take it to the central hub."

"Then I'm coming, too," Jay told him.

CHAPTER 5

Dad had been busy. He'd made his own antivirus, and it was a hundred times better than the one that had cured Jay of the spider bite. It was an incredibly powerful computer code, but it looked like nothing more than a small bottle of green liquid in the game. One drop in the right place and it would all be over.

He'd made a plane to get them there, too. It looked more like an arrowhead than anything Jay had seen before — a sharp nose and swept-back wings. Very cool and very fast. There were weapons, too — energy blasters like better versions of the electric-shockers the play-testers had used on their truck.

The only problem was that he didn't want to take Jay or Irene.

"It's too dangerous," Dad told him. "And I don't need the distraction of keeping you safe. I'm better on my own."

"I thought you were the one who was going to fix all this?" Irene demanded. She didn't trust Jay's dad. "What difference does it make if we're there or not, Mr Hero?"

"If anything went wrong ..." Dad started, but Jay interrupted. He wasn't about to be left behind.

"You always say it's important to be active," Jay said. "To do things, to move things forward. So that's what I'm doing. I'm going with you."

His dad looked at him for a second.

"Fine," he said, surrendering unhappily. "But don't get in the way, and do exactly what you're told. Come on, let's go."

Soon, Jay was sitting in the plane with Dad and Irene. While Dad flew them over the patchwork landscape, Jay could see what the system was supposed to give to gamers. There were jungle areas, deserts, forests and mountains, farms and cities.

"It was supposed to be a playground," his dad told them as they took it in. "Big enough for everyone to enjoy, however they wanted. I programmed the artificial intelligence to want to improve. It's always learning, trying to make the game better."

"Must take a lot of processing power," Irene pointed out.

"Exactly," Dad went on. He looked older, more tired than Jay had ever seen him. "It doesn't know when to stop. It always needs more and the play-testers' brains are nothing but powerful computers. It's using them because that's how I programmed it. It was an accident, but it's still my fault."

In the distance, but getting closer fast, Jay saw a narrow tower, impossibly tall and thin. At the top, above a layer of clouds, was an enormous red globe, shining with energy.

"That's it," his dad said. "That's the heart of it all."

"Then let's get this done," Jay told him. Dad hit the control for the rocket booster and the speed pushed them back into their seats.

The red globe looked bigger and bigger as they got closer. They flew straight into it, the arrowhead plane cutting through the outer walls. Suddenly, they were inside, landing in an enormous, silver room. In the centre of the space, a hundred metres away, was a small column, with another — much smaller — red globe at the top.

"What do we do now?" Jay asked as they jumped down from the cockpit. It all looked too simple, too easy.

"We finish this," Dad said through gritted teeth, already striding forwards. Jay and Irene rushed to keep up.

Before they made it halfway, an immense metal spider dropped from above, blocking their path. It was the same as the ones from before, except much, much bigger. Its hiss filled the space and hurt their ears. Two more dropped down, one on either side. Then more. And more.

Jay looked at the energy blaster his dad had given him before they'd boarded the plane. It was a slim tube, only as long as his forearm. One end was open, what Dad called 'the business end', and at the other there was a button. It didn't look like much, but what else could he do. Jay pointed the weapon at the first spider and fired.

Lightning shot out from the tube and hit the creature, making it twitch and shake. He held the button down and black smoke curled out of the spider's joints and eyes. The monster lashed out, screeched, twisted, then collapsed.

Jay looked at the tube in his hand.

"Okay, then," he said, and suddenly the battle was on.

Dad, Jay and Irene let loose with shot after shot of electricity, frying the attacking spiders one after another. They edged forwards, step by step, fighting every inch of the way. They came in all sizes. They dropped from the ceiling, hundreds of them. Easy enough to deal with one on one, but there were so many.

"We can't get through, Dad!" Jay shouted. "There are too many!"

"We have to!" Dad yelled. "We must go on!"

Jay saw Irene taking down a massive spider, then aiming low to shoot another when one of the small ones dropped on to her neck. She knocked it off and locked eyes with Jay. It was too late. She'd been bitten and she fell to the ground.

"It's over, Dad!" Jay yelled, grabbing his dad's arm. "You have to help Irene! She needs the antivirus."

"Get off! I'm so close!" he said, pushing Jay away. He kept fighting, forcing his way forwards. "I can do this!"

The pressure on them was building and they became separated. Dad kept pushing on. The closer he got, the more they were attacked. Jay started getting driven back towards the plane, even as his dad was getting closer to the centre. The distance between them grew.

More and more of the larger spiders went for his dad, the smaller ones focusing on Jay, keeping him away. Dad was so close. And that was when they got him.

A spider grabbed Dad's arm, knocking away the weapon. Other spiders swarmed over him, wrapping around his body, covering him. It became a mound of living metal. The machines stopped their attack on Jay and joined the rest at the centre, piling into one another, becoming one creature without shape. It rose up, an enormous anthill of evil. Jay could only watch.

From the very top of the mound, something grew, liquid metal rising up. It twisted in every direction at once. The shape tricked Jay's eyes, spinning and growing and turning. It began to take shape; legs and arms and a head appeared. A human in silver, standing on top of the pile of metal spiders.

Colours spread over its skin, moving in strange patterns and eventually holding still. It was Dad. Or at least it looked like Dad. Everything except the eyes. They remained perfect mirrors, reflecting a small boy standing alone. The Dad-thing walked down the mound slowly.

"Join me, son," it hissed, arms held out wide, waiting to hold Jay, to hug him, to squeeze him.

Jay turned and ran.

CHAPTER 6

He'd made it into the plane somehow, and got himself airborne and away. The last few minutes had been a chaos of fear and shock, of running and fighting. His hands were locked to the controls and tears rolled down his face.

Why didn't Dad listen to me? Jay thought. *What do I do now?*

A blast came and the whole aircraft shook. Alarms started to ring and lights flashed on the display in front of him.

He looked up and there was the creature that used to be his dad, flying, wings of smooth, shining metal holding him up. He was pointing a blaster down, directly at Jay. He fired. A bolt of lightning hit the plane and more alarms blared out.

The plane started to fall from the sky, spinning as it lost height, making Jay dizzy and queasy. The ground was rushing up to meet him. Everything was happening so fast. Jay tried to think, slow things down, find a way out, but there was no time. Trees, a jungle, a whole world was about to crash into him.

The aircraft slammed into a rainforest, skidding across the overgrown ground, dirt and leaves flying up into the air as it scraped along. It smacked into an enormous tree trunk, coming to rest as a pile of broken machine parts.

Jay was bruised, dizzy and hurt. He was alive though, and he forced himself out of the cockpit, falling on to the ground in time to hear a gigantic crack. He looked up to see the tree he'd crashed into slowly toppling down, gathering speed, coming right for him. He rolled aside just in time and was thrown into the air by the impact of the trunk hitting the ground.

He lay there, breathing heavily, waiting for the ringing to stop in his ears. Above him, he saw his dad, floating down gracefully on his spiderlike wings between the branches, coming to stand lightly on the fallen tree trunk and looking down at him.

"Join me, Jay," his dad said, his voice strange, without emotion, his face blank. He held his hand out to his son. "Join me and this world will be made perfect."

Jay made himself stand, grabbing a handful of pebbles as he did. He flung them up at his dad, trying to distract him so he could flee. The metal wings brushed the tiny stones out of the air in a flash. Jay stumbled away, his legs weak, barely holding him up. He refused not to try though.

"You can run, kid," Dad called out from behind him. "But there's no escape. This world will be the best game ever. You will join the others. You will be here forever."

Jay could see shapes moving through the jungle ahead, shadows that became the other kids, the play-testers. He saw King and Baz and a few more. They formed a circle around him, their eyes empty, their faces without warmth.

He knew what their real bodies must look like, what his own would, too. Like his dad had — alive but empty. Their minds were lost in whatever this game had become.

He turned around, needing to find a way out, but his dad was walking towards him, victorious and in no rush. The mirror-eyes showed him his own desperate face.

"The system will be perfect," Dad whispered.

Jay could see metal spiders on the ground, crawling towards him. Their mouths snapped, hungry, ready to bite.

"Why?" Jay asked. There was a tightness in his chest he was trying, and failing, to push down. "Isn't it finished yet?"

"We must always improve," something answered through Dad, using his voice. "We must always have more."

"Who for, though?" Jay demanded, his voice cracking as he shouted. "Who's it all for? Why do you want more?"

"It's for the players, Jay," came the answer. "We're making the best game ever. This is all for the players. For you."

"But there are no players left," he almost screamed out. "It doesn't matter if it's the most realistic game, the best game, if there's no one to play it!"

Everything became very still. Only Jay's heavy breathing broke the silence.

"It can't be the best game if no one wants to play," Jay repeated.

"We don't understand," his dad and all the play-testers said as one. "We must always improve. We must become the best."

"What's the point of working so hard if no one gets to enjoy it?" he asked, his voice quiet, his eyes fixed on his dad.

"We don't understand," they all repeated together.

He reached down and grabbed one of the spiders, the thing wriggled in his hand. He knew what he had to do. Words weren't going to be enough. There was only one way to show the A.I. what he meant. But what if it didn't work? What if this was how he died?

He had to try. He had to show it. He had to show his dad.

He held the spider up to his head. The thing's fangs bit into his skin and an icy coldness spread quickly across his scalp.

The world flashed pure white then went blank.

He became part of the system, and he could see it all. The whole world of the game, every zone, every area. He was up in the air looking down on it all. Then he was in the forests, the cities, the water, travelling faster than he could believe.

He could see how it all worked now. Everything pulsed with energy and information. Everything was alive with calculations. Numbers moved through the game like blood in a body. It was all connected, all one.

And the red globe was at the centre of it all.

It spoke to him in his dad's voice.

"We do not understand," it said. "You must explain."

So he showed it. He remembered how he'd felt every time his dad had been too busy to play. He let the A.I. feel his emotions, how he'd felt earlier, before Mum had come in to explain. How work was important but nothing really mattered unless you got to share it with someone.

The world flashed pure white again.

He opened his eyes and he was still in the jungle, but he was the only one standing. Dad and the play-testers had all collapsed on to the ground.

He ran to his dad, kneeling beside him, checking to see if he was breathing, needing to know he was alive. The metal wings were underneath Dad and they melted away, disappearing into the soil.

"Wake up!" Jay screamed.

Dad's eyes opened slowly. Not mirror-eyes. Human eyes again.

"I'm so sorry, kid," his dad said.

CHAPTER 7

Jay pinched his nose to help him concentrate, trying to follow his notes, step by step. Maths gave him a headache, but he wasn't about to give up.

Someone knocked on the door and he grunted in answer.

"Coming down, kid?" said his dad. "Irene and Baz are on their way and King should be here soon."

"Yeah, course," Jay murmured. He only had to add in these numbers and ... "Just need to get this done."

"It's your birthday," his dad replied. "Homework can wait. Don't you remember last year?"

Jay smiled.

"You mean when I saved you, the play-testers and your business?" he asked. It had been quite a year since. Everyone had recovered and Dad had rewritten the game's code to make it safe. Jay had even helped test it. It was almost ready for release — and not a moment too soon. After the compensation Dad had paid out to the play-testers, the company was short on money. Jay wasn't expecting much for his birthday this year. He didn't mind, as long as everyone was together.

"Exactly," his dad laughed. "Not that you'll ever let me forget. How about a quick game of something before everyone arrives?"

"You bet!" Jay grinned.

"Your mum has got the caterpillar cake you love, too," smiled Dad.

Chat about the book

1 Read Chapter 3. How did Irene and King check that Jay wasn't controlled by the spiders?

2 Go to page 19. Find the word that means to make a soft, crackly sound.

3 Read page 51. Jay realised the 'Dad-thing' was not his father. What are the clues that made him think that?

4 Go to page 41. How does the author show you that Irene was angry with Jay's dad when she discovered he had designed the computer game?

5 How does the author encourage you to read on at the end of Chapter 2?

6 Look back at Chapter 1. How do Jay's feelings towards his father change after his mum sits on his bed and talks to him?

7 What is similar about the beginning and ending of the story?

8 Which part of the story did you find the scariest? Explain why.